THE SELF-CONTROL PATROL WORKBOOK: EXERCISES FOR ANGER MANAGEMENT

by Terry Trower
Illustrated by Bruce Van Patter

The Center for Applied Psychology, Inc.
King of Prussia, Pennsylvania

The Self-Control Patrol Workbook: Exercises for Anger Management
by Terry Trower
Illustrated by Bruce Van Patter

Published by:
The Center for Applied Psychology, Inc.
P.O. Box 61587, King of Prussia, PA 19406 U.S.A.
Tel. 1-800-962-1141

The Center for Applied Psychology, Inc., is the publisher of Childswork/Childsplay, a catalog of products for mental health professionals, teachers, and parents who wish to help children with their social and emotional growth.

Second Printing

© Copyright 1995 by The Center for Applied Psychology, Inc.
Printed in the United States of America.

ISBN# 1-882732-38-3

THE SELF-CONTROL PATROL WORKBOOK

Self-control is an important attribute for all children to develop, but particularly children with Attention Deficit Disorders with Hyperactivity (ADHD) or other behavioral problems. While these children almost always benefit from behavioral programs, these programs do not teach children the inner controls that are necessary to social success and improved academic performance.

The Self-Control Patrol Workbook is designed to make learning self-control skills fun! Included in the workbook, you will find more than 50 activities designed to:

- Teach the value of self-discipline.
- Teach children to anticipate the consequences of their behavior.
- Teach children to communicate their thoughts and feelings instead of acting them out.
- Teach children the importance of following rules.
- Teach children the effect that their behavior has on others.
- and much more.

The Self-Control Patrol Workbook is designed to be a part of a complete therapeutic program for impulsive children or children having behavioral difficulties. The activities are designed as "therapeutic homework" to give children the extra time to think and learn about self-control issues.

ANGER ASSESSMENT

1. What usually makes you angry?

Write it below

_____

_____

_____

_____

_____

_____

1

2. How does your body feel when you get angry? (Check all that apply to you.)

 Tight Jaw

 Tears

 Hot Face

 Tight Muscles

 Shallow Breathing/ Dizzy

 Speeding Heart Rate

 Clenched Fist

 Feelings of Confusion

2

3. Draw a picture of your body when you are angry. Color in red the parts of your body where you feel the anger.

BEHAVIOR

4. What do you usually do when you get angry? (Check all that may apply.)

____ Pretend that I'm not angry

____ Use the silent treatment

____ Call names

____ Tease

____ Insult and make smart remarks

____ Talk about someone's mother

____ Talk behind someone's back

____ Yell

____ Push, shove, or kick

____ Bite

____ Use obscene gestures

____ Curse

____ Threaten

____ Hit

____ Slam doors

____ Throw things

5. Draw a cartoon showing an angry situation in your life.

What made me angry.

What I said and did.

What happened next.

CONSEQUENCES

6. Do you get in trouble when you lose your temper?

____ at home?

____ at school?

Write a story about a boy or girl who lost his or her temper below.

_____

_____

_____

_____

_____

_____

_____

_____

_____

_____

_____

_____

_____

_____

_____

_____

7. Who is in this picture below? Complete the picture showing what happens when you get in trouble for losing your temper.

(You)   (_____)

8. How do you feel after you get in trouble? (Circle all that apply.)
Write about a time when you had each feeling.

Scared

Mad

Sad

_____
_____
_____
_____

_____
_____
_____
_____

_____
_____
_____
_____

Lonely

Guilty

_____
_____
_____
_____

_____
_____
_____
_____

9. What privileges do you lose when you get in trouble at home?

_____

_____

_____

_____

_____

_____

What happens when you get in trouble at school?

_____

_____

_____

_____

_____

_____

10. How would you feel about yourself if you didn't get in trouble as often?

_____

_____

_____

_____

_____

Draw a picture of how things would be different.

11. **Would you be willing to try some new behaviors to help you stay out of trouble?**

Yes   No   Not Sure

If you marked either "Yes" or "Not Sure," then

(You may go to the next page.)

If you marked "No," take a 24-hour break and come back tomorrow.

ANGER AWARENESS QUIZ

Mark "T" for True and "F" for False.

____ 1. Anger is a bad emotion.

____ 2. Only bad people get angry.

____ 3. Some people cannot control their anger.

____ 4. It is helpful to try to ignore angry feelings.

____ 5. Once you get angry, there is nothing you can do to calm down.

ANGER FACTS

(To be read aloud)

1. False. Anger is not a bad emotion. Anger is a normal emotion.

2. False. If I am normal, I will feel angry at times. Every human being experiences anger. My mom, dad, brother, sister, teacher, principal, and best friend all feel anger sometimes.

3. False. Angry feelings can always be controlled. If I don't know how to control my anger, I can find out by asking a parent, teacher, counselor, or friend.

4. False. Ignoring my angry feelings is like squeezing one end of a balloon. The anger simply moves to another location, but it always comes back, sometimes when I least expect it.

5. False. Once I am angry, I can activate an "anger plan" to calm myself down. If I plan in advance, I'll know what to do.

Read the above facts again standing up.

Read them sitting down.

Read them in a whisper.

How many can you remember without looking?

ANGER IS A SIGNAL THAT. . .

1. I am being hurt or threatened. . .

14

2. Someone I care about is being hurt or threatened. . .

3. Something I care about is being hurt or threatened. . .

Anger warns me that something doesn't feel right.

Draw a picture showing how you would react
to being hurt or threatened.

A car that is in control can take you many places. . .

A car out of control rarely reaches
its destination. . .
Therefore, it is important to stay
in control.

What type of "control" car are you? _____

Draw a car that represents you below.

THE POWER OF WORDS

Can you recall receiving a compliment? If so, write it below.

_____

_____

How does it make you feel?

_____

_____

Can you recall something unkind that was said to you? Write it below.

_____

_____

How does it make you feel?

_____

_____

WORDS are POWERFUL.
They have the power to HURT or HEAL.

"I" Messages state how you truly feel without blaming, insulting, threatening, or calling names.

"You" Messages usually involve blaming, threatening, or name-calling.

"I" Message

I want you to save me a seat on the bus.

"You" Message

You'd better save me a seat on the bus or you'll be sorry.

If these statements were said to you, how would you respond?

_____   _____

_____   _____

_____   _____

_____   _____

_____   _____

"Power Talk" is another effective way to communicate your feelings in a way that doesn't insult or blame.

For example:

NOTICE!!! No blaming. No name-calling. No insults. No threats.

Now, you try:

When you _____

I Feel _____ Because _____

Please _____

or

I get mad when you _____

Because _____

Please _____

POWER TALK RERUN

Do you remember the last time you were angry?

Suppose you could rerun the scene using Power Talk. Write down what you would say below.

Describe what happened.

_____

_____

_____

_____

Now use Power Talk.

_____

_____

_____

_____

Power Talk can also be used to communicate <u>Positive</u> feelings.

Power Talk Works!

Draw a cartoon of yourself using Power Talk with your best friend.

SELF-CONTROL SHORELINE

Christopher Codfish is minding his own business when he is suddenly approached by the menacing scavenger, Sidney Shark.

1.

Suddenly Sidney throws him a hook, loaded with the enticing bait.

2.

3.

What is Christopher to do? (Put a check next to your answer.)

_____ (a) Take the bait and jump on the hook.

_____ (b) Swim away to peaceful waters.

_____ (c) Use an "I" Message.

_____ (d) Counterattack with a "You" Message.

_____ (e) Use Power Talk.

_____ (f) Faint.

4. Draw a picture of what will happen next.

5. REMEMBER:
Don't be shark bait.
Don't be dinner.
Swim away. And be a winner.

INTERVIEW

Your assignment is to interview someone in your life whose self-control you admire. This interviewee may be an adult or a peer.

Name of Interviewee: _____

1. How do you control your temper?

_____

_____

_____

2. What do you do when other people aggravate you?

_____

_____

_____

3. What do you see me doing that might cause others to want to aggravate me?

_____

_____

_____

4. (Question of your choice.)

_____

_____

_____

5. What do you advise me to do when I start to feel angry?

_____

_____

_____

Anger gets stuck in the body. Simply using a calming technique or ignoring someone will not get rid of the anger (although it will keep you out of trouble).

The best way to dissolve your angry feelings is through vigorous exercise. Which form of exercise appeals to you? (Check all that apply.)

___ Taking Deep Breaths

___ Fast Walking

___ Riding My Bike

___ Football

___ Baseball

___ Soccer

___ Cheerleading

___ Jumping Rope

___ Track

___ Lifting Weights

___ Martial Arts

___ Rollerblading

___ Swimming

___ Other _____

Whew! I feel better now!

32

SHRINK THE PICTURE

I. Draw a picture of something that makes you mad, angry, or sad every time you think about it.

Picture A

2. Color the picture with bright, vibrant colors.
3. If there is conversation in the picture, is it loud or soft?

4. Now draw the same picture, using only a pencil, in the tiny space provided below.

Picture B

5. Every time you think of the upsetting scene (Picture A), shrink the size of the picture in your mind to the size of Picture B.

If there are voices in the picture, turn down the volume to a whisper. Close your eyes and try to shrink the picture to the size of a postage stamp.

Can you do it?

DAILY PERSONAL PEACE PLAN

(From the list below, choose a different strategy on each of five days. Then decide with an adult which strategy works best for you.)

When I Am Angry Today, I Will:

_____ Ignore the person(s).

_____ Walk away (or take my attention away).

_____ Remind myself of the consequences of losing my temper.

_____ Talk to an adult.

_____ Talk to a friend.

_____ Use Power Talk:
I was mad when you _____
Because _____
Please _____

_____ Distract myself by doing schoolwork.

_____ Distract myself by engaging in something fun.

_____ Dissolve my anger by exercising.

SOCIAL SKILLS

Place a check beside any behaviors that are typical for you.

Friendship Meter

_____ Being Honest

_____ Playing Together

_____ Showing Kindness

_____ Allowing Space/Time Apart

_____ Helping/Sharing

_____ Returning What You Borrow

_____ Talking About Feelings

_____ Using "I" Messages

_____ Being Able to Say "No"

_____ Not Believing Messengers

_____ Keeping Promises

_____ Knowing Your Own Strengths

Place a check beside whichever of these you've caught yourself doing.

Problem Meter

____ Breaking Promises

____ Being Possessive/Jealous

____ Not Spending Time
Together

____ Being Dishonest

____ Hiding Your True
Feelings

____ Being a Messenger

____ Spreading Gossip and
Rumors

____ Using "You"
Messages (Blaming)

____ Using the Silent
Treatment

____ Being Late

____ Name-Calling/Insulting

____ Threatening

____ Hitting

D
A
N
G
E
R

Z
O
N
E

HAVING SOCIAL SKILLS IS LIKE A "PROTECTIVE SHIELD" AGAINST ANGER.

39

Write the social skills you have mastered in this jar.

Write the social skills you still need to practice in this jar.

41

JOURNALIZING

Writing feelings down is an excellent way to deal with both comfortable and uncomfortable feelings. When keeping a journal, it is important that you be totally honest. Then you can either share your journal, hide your journal, or throw it away. Writing your feelings down is like talking to a trusted friend.

Dear Journal,

_____

_____

_____

_____

_____

_____

_____

_____

_____

_____

_____

_____

_____

_____

_____

FEELINGS TOSS

Toss a penny onto this page. When it lands on a feeling word, describe a time when you experienced that feeling.

Angry	Sad	Happy	Loving
Confused	Nervous	Jealous	Amused
Worried	Scared	Excited	Compassionate
Frustrated	Hopeful	Hopeless	Lonely

Which feelings do you usually share? _____

With whom: _____

Which feelings do you keep to yourself? _____

44

WATCH YOUR THOUGHTS

Thoughts come before feelings.
Thoughts cause feelings.

For example:

Thought. . .

He gave me a dirty look. Nobody looks at me like that and gets away with it!

Feeling: Angry
What do you think he will do next?

_____

45

Thought. . .

He gave me a dirty look. I don't like that, but maybe he's having a bad day.

Feeling: Irritated/Confused

What do you think he will do next?

_____

_____

_____

What do you tell yourself before you get angry?

_____

_____

_____

What could you say to yourself instead?

_____

_____

_____

THINGS I TELL MYSELF

Now Hear This. . .

Put a check beside each statement that you believe is true about yourself.

1. ____ I'm stupid.
2. ____ I'm ugly.
3. ____ Other kids are more talented than I am.
4. ____ I'm no good at sports.
5. ____ Nobody pays attention to what I do.
6. ____ Nobody pays attention to what I say.
7. ____ Nobody likes me.
8. ____ I'm a loser.
9. ____ I'll probably fail.
10. ____ If I don't win, I'm no good.
11. ____ I have to go first.
12. ____ People will like me better if I'm tough.
13. ____ People should always agree with what I think.

MY AFFIRMATIONS

Using the numbers that you checked on the previous page, ask an adult to help you complete each statement. In this way, you can practice changing your negative self-talk and you will feel less angry and more hopeful.

1. _____ is hard for me but I would improve if I _____.

2. I don't like my_____. But I do like my _____ _____.

3. I would like to develop a talent in _____. I could begin to work on this by _____.

4. I need more practice in _____(or) what I really like to do is _____.

5. Whose attention do I want? _____.
I can get it by _____.

6. Who do I want to listen to me? _____.
The person has time to listen when _____.

7. My friend _____ likes me.

8. I can learn from mistakes. I've learned that _____ _____.

9. I can pass if I _____.

10. If I don't win, I can still have a lot of fun playing _____.

11. I'm important whether I'm first or _____.

12. It's better to be liked than _____.

13. What I think is okay. What you think is okay. I don't have to convince you and you don't have to convince me. It's okay to have different _____. We're both okay.

48

MORE ABOUT ME

OK, so I get angry. Now what?

1. Three things I like about myself are:

_____

_____

_____

2. Two things I would like to change about myself are:

_____

_____

3. My favorite subject in school is _____
and I make my best grades in _____

4. My favorite year in school was (is) _____
because _____

5. My favorite sport or hobby is _____

6. I feel safe telling my real feelings to _____
because _____

7. When I grow up, I would like to _____

_____

49

VALUES SURVEY

Which is important to you?
Rank from 1 - 6 (1=most important and 6=least important)

_____ Making my parents proud of me.

_____ Knowing I've done a good job.

_____ Hearing compliments about my achievements.

_____ Getting awards (certificates, etc.).

_____ Winning (knowing I've done better than someone else).

_____ Other _____

Parent Recognition Statement

I hereby recognize and value the fact that my child,

_____ ,

is motivated by _____ .

Signed, _____

Parent Signature

HOW AM I DOING NOW?

Fill out the following worksheet for seven consecutive days to practice your new self-control skills.

I Lost Control Today By:	M	T	W	Th	F	Sat	Sun
Name-Calling							
Insulting/Teasing							
Threatening							
Pushing							
Hitting							
Other							
I Used Self-Control This Week By:							
Ignoring/Walking Away							
Counting to 10							
Taking Deep Breaths							
Talking to a Friend							
Talking to an Adult							
Using "I" Messages							
Using Power Talk							
Writing in My Journal							
Drawing							
Exercising							
Doing Something Fun							

Are You Still Angry? (Circle One)   Yes   No

If yes, what do you need to do now?

_____

_____

_____

MY FAVORITE ANIMAL

Draw your favorite animal below.

1. I chose this animal because

_____

_____

2. Two things I admire about this animal are

_____

_____

3. I am like this animal because

_____

_____

53

"MY HERO"

1. Who is your hero? Who do you admire? Write his or her name down.

_____

2. Circle the characteristics of your hero.

Generous   Strong

    Intelligent   Kind

       Affectionate   Helpful

   Fun-Loving   Sensitive

         Athletic

Responsible   Talented

   Trustworthy   Attractive

Friendly   Loving

      Funny   Adventurous

Thoughtful   Brave

          Caring

3. Is there anything else about your hero which was not included above?

_____

4. Place a double circle around the characteristics of your hero that you have also. Then list them below. I am:

_____

_____

_____

Draw a picture of you with your hero.

WHAT'S GOOD ABOUT ME?

Ask six people to describe your best qualities. Write them below.

Mother _____

_____

Father _____

_____

Brother / Sister _____

_____

Teacher _____

_____

Friend _____

_____

Your Choice _____

_____

I'M A STAR

Looking back at pages **54-56**, fill in the sections of the star with the things you like about yourself. These are the ways in which you "shine."

"I'm as unique as each individual star that shines brightly in the evening sky."

PROBLEM-SOLVING WORKSHEET

Sometimes having problems on your mind can really put you "on edge. . ."

"I've got this problem and I'm feeling on edge."

1. What is your problem? _____

_____

_____

2. What have you done to solve it? _____

_____

3. Find some friends/adults to help you brainstorm other ideas that you might try. Then write these ideas below.

_____

_____

4. For each idea, write why you like it (+). Is there any reason you don't (-).

_____

_____

5. Which idea looks the best to you now? #_____. Try this out and report back on the results.

6. The result was

_____

_____

7. Do you need to try another solution? (circle one)   **Yes   No**

STUDY SKILLS CHECKLIST

Study skills are an important part of feeling in control and keeping up with assignments. Circle the study skills below that apply to you.

Classwork

1. I have my book, pencil, and paper.	Yes	No
2. I look at my teacher when she/he is talking.	Yes	No
3. I listen to directions.	Yes	No
4. I ask for help if I don't understand.	Yes	No
5. I begin my assignment on time.	Yes	No
6. I finish and turn in my assignments.	Yes	No
7. I write down my homework assignment.	Yes	No

Homework

1. I do my homework in a quiet place.	Yes	No
2. I leave my books, backpack, etc. in a special place so I don't forget them.	Yes	No
3. I turn in my homework.	Yes	No

Tests

1. I read over the material the night before the test.	Yes	No
2. I call out questions to myself or have someone call them out to me.	Yes	No
3. I go to bed on time.	Yes	No
4. I take three deep breaths before the test.	Yes	No

Circle the skills to which you answered "no." If, through practice, you can change these to a "yes," notice what happens to both your feelings of success and your gradepoint. They'll go up.

59

SELF-CONTROL CROSSWORD

Using the information you have learned about self-control and anger management, complete the crossword puzzle with the clues provided below.

Across

1. A way to communicate your feelings without insulting or blaming.
6. You are _____; another word for "special."
8. A furry best friend who won't talk back.
10. A way to communicate your feelings so that others will listen.
11. A way to learn how fictional characters handle problems.
12. A helping adult who assists you in solving problems and handling feelings.
14. "_____ calling" is insulting.
15. "_____, look, and listen" is a way to think about your choices when angry.
16. A way to have fun; the opposite of work.
18. The opposite of angry.
19. Someone who attends an elementary or middle school.
20. Those with a sense of _____ don't get angry as often.
21. An adult listener at school.
22. A put-down.
23. Using this social skill is the "best policy."
25. A free-wheeling form of exercise.
27. A martial art that teaches self-control.
28. A better way to learn things than by talking.
29. Saying "please" and "thank you."
34. A splashy form of exercise that can help you relax.
35. Others who like you just the way you are.
36. What some do when they raise their voices.

Down

1. A positive response when others call you names or insult you.
2. A good place to walk when you're angry.
3. A physical way to drain anger out of your body.
4. Another word for "diary."
5. A method to calm yourself down: "Take three _____ and call me in the morning."
7. An adult in your home who may be able to help you solve problems.
9. When angry, count to _____.
12. A way to distract yourself when angry.
13. A consequence of fighting at school.
14. Just say "_____" to fighting.
17. A "_____" message indicates blame.
18. Keep your _____.
24. When you lose this, you're really angry.
27. Everyone desires to be treated with _____.
28. A way to lose a friend's trust; the opposite of telling the truth.
32. You can never have too many of these.
33. A great place to record your feelings.

Answers on page 63

Self-Control Patrol Club

This is to certify that

_____

has successfully completed the course and is an honorary member of the "Self-Control Patrol."

As a member, you must serve as an example to others!

Terry Trower
Guidance Counselor

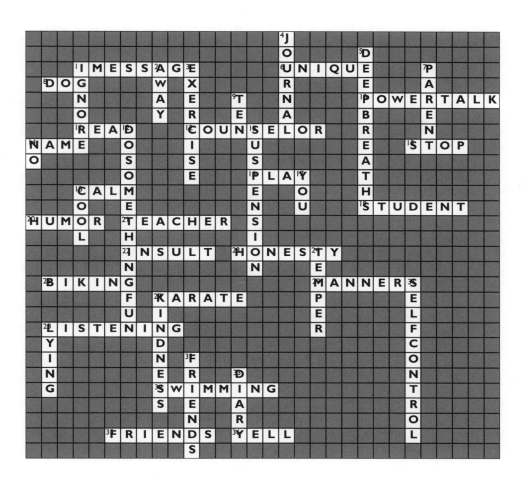